Parts of Me

Tanishi Agarwal

ISBN 979-8-89026-915-7

To Sree Laxmi ma'am, thank you for teaching me that writing can be so much more than mere words.

"Don't limit poetry to the word. Poetry can be found in music, a photograph, in the way a meal is prepared—anything with the stuff of revelation in it. It can exist in the most everyday things, but it must never, never be ordinary. By all means, write about the sky or a girl's smile, but when you do, let your poetry conjure up salvation day, doomsday, any day. I don't care, as long as it enlightens us, thrills us and—if it's inspired—makes us feel a bit immortal."

– N.H. Kleinbaum, Dead Poets Society

Contents

Exit As We Enter

From womb to tomb,
We exit as we enter–
Suffocated.
It's a funny thing actually,
We enter unable to express ourselves
And even after years of education,
We cease to express ourselves.

We exit as we enter–
Crying.
When we leave, we realize
Its been years since we came
Yet we still haven't lived at all.
Though we may not cry this time,
Our souls remain devoid of joy

Though I hope,
I'll exit as I entered–
In the embrace of those I loved
And those I never got the time to love.

How Long?

At the tender age of 9, the young child is differentiated on
the basis of colours.

At 11, when everything seems a mess, he is told he can't
cry.

At 13, society expects her to cover up because it was
'distracting,' or 'inappropriate.'

At 15, they are expected to follow certain ambitions
already decided for them.

At 17, he is told to be a man when he is struggling to be
anyone in the first place.

At 19, she is expected to be home earlier than her brother.

At 21, stuck in a world of blue and pink, they struggle to
match the long-set expectations.

At 23, they get married, but not to the person they loved
but the person their parents chose.

At 25, she replaces the barbie in her son's hand with a car.

At 27, he is scared to let his teenage daughter out.

So years later, their kids teach others to be who they want
to be.

If I Can't Have Him

Every night, before sleeping
I think of him
If I can't have him in real life
At least this way, I'll be with him in my dreams.

Everyday I match my steps with him
And say the things he always says
In hopes that if I can't have him
At least I'll become more like him

This way, he'll finally see
How well we go together.
Cause even if I can't have him
I made him the music of my soul.

He's a poem scratched along the walls of my heart
I'll immortalise him through my words
The legacy he bought will forever be etched together in
    these pages
These stories will be heavy with the love we carried.

Cause in the end, even if I can't have him
He never lingered away from my heart.

Parts of Me

There's a heaviness I seem to carry around everywhere
As the day bleeds into nights
And sense blurs into nothingness
It's even tougher to bear the burden of it.

It weighs me down until I'm on the ground
It suffocates me and traps me in my own mind.
It's a drowsy, tiring thing to carry
It slowly consumes me until it becomes a part of me.

It leaves me with no energy, no will to live
Only enough energy to loathe it but not fight it.
It leaves a sense of numbness lingering behind,
Like loud, powerful tides silenced down to gentle waves.

Death's Mockery

She was a bittersweet kindness,
Her eyes soft and tired, with a rough smile.

She was tinted, old memories,
Loud laughter paired with whispers.

She was a wild melancholia–
Made jokes about her despair.

A fiery, hidden thing she was
But she was dying.

Her flames slowly burning out
Her desires mocked by a slow death.

She lived in traps of memories,
Memories slowly fading away.

A deadly thing she was
But alas, death levelled her too.

And now? Now it's attached to her;
It won't let her go.

Nothing

Grinning till our jaws became sore
Cause laughing made our stomachs hurt
Our eyes were glossy with tears,
But you know, the good ones this time.
We were high on coffee
And ridiculous jokes that made us go breathless.

Senseless anecdotes were just an excuse
To cheat sleep for a while longer
Cause nights were when we truly lived
In blinking neon lights and
Flashing streaks of torches,
We lived as though we were immortal.

Murmurs of muffled laughter, paired with
Whispers of the nostalgic tunes of our childhood
Which we never seemed to remember completely.
Things which were funny for no reason
Yet we laughed and sang along
Cause what did we have to lose anyway?

Doing nothing with you was everything for me.

A Heart That Was Never Mine

I loved a heart that was never mine

I said I saw stars in his eyes.
I told my friends I was on cloud nine
They warned hope and love are just lies
Said not to love eyes that'd never look into mine

They'd look at me with concern and pity.
Yet I wouldn't stop, I'd cry and whine
And bask in the warmth of his beauty
So they said this warmth won't suffice for this darkness
     of mine.

His smirk mocked my innocence,
His tears sent shivers down my spine.
They explained happiness & love is a tough balance
Yet I fell for a boy who was never mine.

Coffee Minted Kisses

My mind goes blank at the sight of her
It all becomes a fog of images and words
In the warmth of her body beside me
The thought of speaking itches within my throat
Everything I had wanted to say becomes a blur.

It's all a clear picture in my head.
Her glossy eyes that shine behind her glasses
Her black nails glimmering as they drag across my skin
Her ring scratches along my hands and
Oh, just to lean down and brush against that damn smile.

And like those cliché novels
And romcoms with unrealistic ends,
If you stripped the whole world away from us
We'd still have these bittersweet days
With these coffee-minted kisses to keep us up.

Why

When I was younger,
I wrote poems on irrational questions
Questioning why the sky was blue,
But this? This is something new.

I wonder, I really wonder why
I have to be careful of every guy?
Why I can't wander around without fear?
Why all this, just because I'm a girl?

Why I have to cover up when you're the one distracted?
Why I have to pay for the way you acted?
Why I get punished when you're sexualizing me?
Why, even after being the same as you are, am I not free?

Why do we even have to fight for basic human rights?
Why, after so much, do we still have more fights?
Why are we not valid?
Why does being a girl make you invalid?

Why is pepper spray illegal but not rape?
Why is self-defense punished but not rape?
Why do we have 'be safe' lessons but not lessons on 'don't
    rape?'
Why does the government ignore our questions?

Why by now isn't every country a safe nation?
Why does a thirteen-year-old me understand more than
    most of the population?
Why won't this patriarchy end?
We're tired.

Blind Eyes

Did these scars express it to you?
Or do you still remain oblivious,
Clueless to my grief?
Even after all this time,
Do you only appreciate the bliss of summer?
Ceasing to acknowledge the cold I experience?

Do you believe these grins,
Blatantly ignoring the water reflected in my eyes?
When you hear my laughter,
Do you hear the screams behind?

Or should I internalise this conflict?
Until you start noticing for the first time,
Cause it's been years, and you've only ever viewed me
But never seen, never noticed.
All of me just blends into the background
Blurring amongst the various, unnoticed things

They say beauty lies in the eyes of the beholder,
But the beauty your eyes find, isn't reflected elsewhere
For you, it's all just the warm summer days,
Never the cold nights of these antsy days.

Why I Love You

I love you
Not because I love who you are & how you make me feel
But because I love keeping my mind busy with you
Because you're the only thing that can numb this pain

I love you
Because it's the only thing I've ever known
Because loving you is the only way I can love myself
And I love you because I don't know how not to

7 Billion People – 1 Ideology

The whole world is suffering
Working hard to be someone else
Everyone is doing the same damn thing
Everyone is running behind wealth

They're all like dumb mannequins
Standing still like corpses
With a blank mind and a numb heart
So still, you don't even know they're there.

They don't realize
No one's going to ask them
Their exam results or bank balance
They're all just some numbers

No one cares about any of that
They're too busy in themselves
Busy surviving, existing; so much so
That they forget to live

Cameras

Cameras don't do justice to her
They cease to capture her beauty
They fail to intake her grace.

The wild oceans in her often dull eyes,
That rare light that's brighter than the sun
Whenever she is fascinated or intrigued.

The contagiousness in her smiles,
That passes around when she dances
Almost like she's playing with gravity.

It fails to capture her hair floating in the air
As she runs from person to person
Trying to find someone who clicks.

The crinkles below her eyes when she's focused,
The redness of her face when she's cold,
And the dimples adorning her smile when she's herself.

All of this goes unnoticed by that stupid device
And when she looks at it—
She's unaware of her beauty too.

A Promise of Protection

He watched as I got hit for what he got applauded for
He listened as they disregarded my interests for the
society's interests
He moved aside as I was shoved into the kitchen when
our relatives arrived
He laughed as they made fun of my appearance
He watched as the world silenced me when I tried to
speak out.

He kept quiet as society silenced my screams
And tried to drill me into a numb, speechless mannequin.
He stood there as I fought my way past the patriarchy.
But when he was questioned–
He suddenly realised sexism exists.

Why didn't he say anything earlier?
Where did his 'bond of love' and stupid 'protection' go?
All he had to do was watch;
Watch as my life crumbled to shambles
And his rose above it all.

After all, he was the man of the family
And I? I was the unfortunate girl.
And you know the funniest thing?
The same man who got offended by a box and a poem
Told the girl, she got offended way too easily by this.

Am I Broken?

They say people have trouble opening up
I struggle to lock my feelings in that box everyone seems
    to own
They say people have trouble caring
I wish I could stop
Am I broken?

They say you can't survive without your parents
I struggle surviving around them
They say home is everything to humans
I don't think I have one
Am I broken?

Am I broken because I refuse to fit in the boxes of life
    meant for us,
The format designed for our personalities?
I struggle to think the way everyone does,
Everyone understands each other
I struggle to understand myself.

So I wonder, am I broken?

Heavy Smiles

It's not like she's an atheist
Cause she prays not when we pass temples
But when we pass ambulances.

They say people don't like talking about their feelings,
She has a hard time containing hers
Trying not to pour herself out to others.

She knows bliss and euphoria but
She knows pain too;
You can see it in her eyes.

In the way she smiles
It's sort of a desperate, tired smile
But a smile nonetheless.

All the World is a Stage

All the world is a stage
And we're mere actors doing our role
Putting up a show for everyone to see

We're like mannequins with masks of emotions
But sometimes emotions dance within us
All this while, we stay blank

Pretending there isn't a war going on
Cause the world is a stage
And we must act to be a part of it

We hide beneath costumes and facades
Waiting for people to realise that it's just a play
An act to cover it up.

We're so engrossed and lost
In the different roles we play
We lose ourselves in this theatre of life.

Seas and the Sky

In a crowd of people, you're the first I see
Yet you pretend like you don't even know me
I'm drowning in thoughts consumed by you.
I'm the goddamn ocean, and you're the part that's blue
Without you, there's no me;
Like no waves, no shores, just the plain sea.

My eyes travel to you
And then, all the fairytale bullshit seems true.
With every breath, you seem even further away.
"Just a look," my damn desperate eyes say
I know just a look is all it would take
But I still look, just for this heart's sake.

Slowly I sink deeper into this pit of love
Cause who cares about the sea when there's a whole damn
   sky above.

Existing

Perhaps we are so afraid to die
That we truly never live at all.
We're so afraid of dying,
Of the moment we'll stop breathing, stop living,
That we stop living altogether.
We suffocate ourselves until the moment
Where we're just existing.

We Grew Up

As the smiles faded and frowns arose
Everything around us changed.

Sleep turned from a punishment
To a reward we rarely ever got.

From drawing portraits to drawing scars,
Our hobbies changed.

Friends, gatherings, and hanging out
Didn't give us joy anymore.

Interlocked hands and hugs
Turned into awkward phone calls and one-word texts

Games didn't mean fun any more,
They meant 'love.'

We all grew close
But only physically

'What happened,' society asked.
'They grew up,' came the answer.

What they didn't hear was the inevitable truth
'You forced us to.'

You, Me and Death

Even my despair is lonely without you
It, too, seeks out the little escapes you provided
The emptiness you cast between us seems unbearable.

Death may have levelled you now
But I swear, your memory will burn in my heart
For as long as it beats

The legacy you left will live on in the poems I write
The days I laugh and nights I cry
The scars I crave will have traces of you

And if I shall die,
I'll die with you in my mind
The thought of reunion to keep my lifeless body company.

Then the doors shall open,
And we'll be together yet again.
The chase between you, me and death no more.

He's Not Coming Back

"He's not coming back."
Yet I wait
Yet I run towards the door
Hoping it's him.

Knowing that smile is never returning.
All I have with him
Are memories now
Memories burned into my heart.

As if it was just yesterday
As if he'll laugh for the last time again
As if his heart will beat again
He will come back.

He'll be here again; with us
Not just as a memory that's
Slowly losing itself
Slowly fading away.

The smile that brought laughter once
Brings tears now.
The flowers on his table once
Are on his grave now.

Reminding us - he's not coming back.

Buried in Silence

The world melting at our fingertips,
The burden of broken promises
Drifting from our shoulders.
In the scarred, trembling nights,
The fire of a billion hearts burn
Along with it cries the bundle of fear and insecurity.

Through the morning till the night,
It whispers its song of reminiscence
Silence weighs it down as
Incomplete words suffer to walk past the crowd.
Of all the times to love each other
This was the most painfully beautiful one

The world around us faded
As we realized;
We were buried in silence.

Shattered Dreams and Stolen Hope

Every dream shattered
Feels like shards of broken glass
Slammed & stomped on
By those who couldn't fulfil theirs.

Every hope stolen from me
Feels like parts of me taken away
And all that remains are hollowed spaces
That have nothing to fill themselves with.

Every thought disregarded enrages me
The way you walk all over them
Ceasing to even acknowledge them
Let alone consider them.

So, don't you dare ask for
The fuel to this constant fire
Don't negotiate this fury with your lazy excuses
This is a lifelong vain, don't try to silence it now.

You have absolutely no rights
To complain about broken dreams and unfateful hopes
Sitting on a throne made of
Our dreams & hopes that you shattered.

Fire

She was unlike any,
She differed so much from me, that we were almost
   similar

You know those girls whose souls burn with passion,
The ones who bear the entire world in their eyes.

To compliment their dirty minds,
They own the brightest fire in their hearts.

Yeah, she was like that,
Wild and fiery with a feisty humour.

Along with her unforgettable smug smirk,
She owned a loud voice if her gait's power didn't suffice.

From ripped jeans to dirty, worn-out sneakers,
From dangling earphones to her scribbled hands

Everything about her screamed 'messy,'
And yet she's the only one who could sort me out.

I met her and it felt like
Fire was discovered for the second time in human history.

No One

I don't have anyone to stick pictures of on my wall
Or to introduce to my family
I don't have anyone to mark their birthday on my calendar
Or make their contact my favourite

I don't have anyone to celebrate Christmas with
Or even kiss on new years
No one to miss me if I'm not here anymore,
No one to even realise I'm not.

Horizon

It's always been a dream of mine
Just to leave everyone, let go of everything
And run towards the horizon
As the sun drowns past it
As a wisp of clouds floats over the distant hill tops
As the whistling of the wind drowns out the bird's melody
In that moment, there'd be no future, no past
Just me and the horizon
The water below my leg would feel like magic
Or perhaps heaven in a parallel universe
The sunset would be reflected in the waves
Or rather my eyes
And the whole world would be chanting the same thing;
"It's beautiful."
So much so, I've forgotten all the words I've learned.

Shit, I Think I Love You

I love you and it scares me
I don't think I've ever loved anyone before
I've shied away from love as long as I can remember.

I love you like old couples love each other
I think of you like little teenage boys do
I fantasise about you like those girls in romcoms do.

I'm afraid I'll love you like my parents love
I'm afraid I'll be like them, and I know I will
Cause its the only thing I've known my entire life.

Secret Smiles

You're a mess of awkward, shy glances
With tears held back and
A sloppy smile spread across

With eyes that clearly show slumber has eluded you
Slurry words stuttered out
Accompanied by the softest giggles.

In the ridiculously adorable clothes you wear
You owned a gait that couldn't be more nonchalant.
You entangled me into a mess of secret smiles.

Dear X

Dear x,

This is a reality check for you. To tell you how these little, seemingly insignificant words still echo in my head.

Dearest x,

It is to remind you of what a hypocrite you are. All the years of abuse and words have clashed into something so inexplicably disturbing that it hollows me and devoids me of any joy.

Dear x,

This is a very friendly reminder that I am not him. I'm not perfect like he is, and it kills me almost as much as it does you.

Dearest x,

This is to tell you that the food that you deprived me of has now become my love-hate conflict. All thanks to you, who else could mess me up like you did? Yet, who else can love me like you do?

Hollowed Memories

This distance seems like an ever-increasing barrier.
As though there's a border between us.

These little moments with you are fading now.
It's hard to remember how we were together.

In this blur, all I know are the days I shivered and cried
    under your terror.
The 'I love yous' and 'I'm proud of yous,' that I chased my
    entire life don't seem so meaningful any more.

I don't miss you you as much anymore:
The knife you dug so deep has been pulled out, and all
    that remains are scars.

Your love is nothing but a memory now.
I love you, but honestly, I never knew you.

Because I Love You

I'm okay
I'm okay when these words won't stop echoing in my head.
I'm okay even when these memories burn into my heart
I'm okay even when everything is broken into pieces
And my body begs to give out.

Cause, I love you.
I love you even when I trace these scars in the dark
I love you when I push my plate away, ignoring my growling
 stomach.
I love you when you sway out of drunkenness and slur
 your words
I love you even when I'm confused about whether I should.

I love you even when I hate you
And for that I hate you
I hate that you believe my 'I am okays,'
I hate that you make me love you
I hate myself even more for hating you cause, really, I love
 you.

The Games We Play

A blur, broken memory
With a slur of words,
The only I haven't forgotten
Is you; standing across the room
A hesitant smile on your face
A soft sway in your words
It was a drunken mess
But you were there, and I was, too,
Living through this mess
Like we could never live again
Freely caged amongst the lies
Amongst the games we play.
Saying we couldn't try
But the truth is:
We didn't want to; even if we could
Even then, you knew my deepest secrets
But not who I really was
And in that way,
Life played with us all.

Darkness and Despair

The distance dawned on me during dawn,
Darkness and despair danced within me.
Dare I say, dangerously demeaning dreams of it have
Daunted me with discomfort almost daily.

December depression dampens my defence
Until I'm dripping with drops of tears
Deep down, a dash of discomfort
Defeats the lack of darkness daily till I break down.

Lost in You

Every night, I laid awake, just so I didn't miss your texts.
7 billion faces and yet I only look for yours
Know we are not talking anymore,
Still take a glance at our place as I walk by

Every day, I re-read your letter;
You said you deserved better
But I still can't believe you left me
Even though you promised we were meant to be.

Every time we ended our conversations
With 'let's meet soon,'
But never ended up meeting.
All these games, and you chose to play with my heart.

Echoes of Terror

An echoing whisper of terror rings out
Hidden beneath the masks and facades
Begging to breakthrough,
Begging to be set free,
Tied together and replaced by a smile instead

It waited for people to realize;
Realize that these are just games
That it's just a play to cover it up
But alas, how can they?
When the creator itself hasn't.

Everyone likes the loud, comic plays
But no one stays for the silence after
It's not like they don't like it
They're just scared, frightened
Again, shadowed by the echoing whispers of terror.

Flower Crowns and Ball Gowns

We danced to classical melodies
In a hall full of balls gowns and flower crowns
We didn't know we were making memories
We just knew we were done with the frowns

I ignored the love and passion dancing within me
We told ourselves, it wasn't true
We kept quiet, but our hearts begged to be free.
All this while our love only grew.

Until it finally happened that night
You came rushing in and held my hand
You pulled me aside and whispered under the moonlight
"Society be dammed."

I was a girl and so were you
But we didn't seem to mind
We didn't think it through
Love had made us blind.

But our definition of love
Wasn't accepted by everyone
Yet, I couldn't care enough
Cause I had found the one.

Silent Words

Shadows blow past with the echoing hollow of the wind. Complete darkness submerges us, bringing along with it the deafening, unbearable silence. Amidst this, the only sound to be heard is the endless horror words running through my mind. It's silent for a while before I realize in this silence it has spoken more than ever.

I cried out for help, but they too were silent, they too were not loud enough to break this facade of silence. Emotion of emotion they all tried, but my tears too were silent. Just as my smile was–quiet and desperate. When nothing worked, they all left. Then it was just me trying to defeat the silence with a crying mind and a numb heart. My numbness loved the silence though, said it made it feel nothing yet everything. In my silence, I agreed.

The only thing that could defeat it was 3 steps forward. So for the last time, I screamed again; the crash overpowered it too.

Lessons of School

Our character is defined
By the length of our skirts
Our worth is defined by our clothes
Tha's what my school taught me.

Our character is who we are
Our worth is what we set it as
Not our clothes, not our friends
Tha's what school failed to teach me

Our personality is defined
By how we adjust to these unjust riles
Without questioning why
Our personality isn't ours to decide,

That's what school taught me.

Whispers

An endless void of monotonous days carries me
I don't know how I got here
But here I am now,
Confused, lost, scared.

In this terrifying whirlpool of emotions
Alone, I stand
Bound by chains and cages
An invisible trap holding me back.

I struggle and I struggle
Until I'm too tired, too fragile
Alone, I fight a demon I can't even see
And only one sound rings through

Whispers, terrifying loud whispers
Whispers that hurt me, shatter me
Run through me like a sword
Cut me deeper than weapons could

Whispers of the dead
Whispers of the helpless, of the silence.
Like death blowing past you,
It whispers.

It whispers till your own thoughts are too soft
Till whispers sound like screams
Till the whispers trap you
Trap you in an endless void.

Whispers, in a way,
Are more dangerous than screams
They work silently
So silently, even the victim doesn't hear them,

Once you do,
They are louder than screams.

That Deathly Smile of Life

Her smile glitters with hope and beauty
Secrets lie deep within her eyes
Even more ethereal, however,
Is the way she speaks
She sounds like a melody playing
Her lies sound prettier than all of our truths

Her fiery spirit lights up the dorm
Igniting the spark of joy she carries around
Her running is like wind passing by
And when she dances,
She is engulfed by the moves
It's almost like she's playing tricks with gravity

All this while, her face is adorned
With a smile ready to kill
A smile you'd never want to let go.

Lost in Lies

I tried pretending like it didn't bother me
I tried playing with emotions
Bending them as I like

Smiling my way through hell
Smiling as a thousand knives struck me
Silencing my screams to smiles

Waking up happy every day
As if yesterday wasn't hell
As today wasn't going to be the same.

I tried covering it up with masks
Pushing it all down so even
I couldn't find it

In this mess of a mind
I try looking for my own thoughts,
Looking for the truth.

But I've covered it too much
I pretended too much
I'm lost in lies now—my own lies.

Grave of Dead Feelings

I feel so much
Yet nothing at the same time
Emotions weigh me down, eat me up
Yet I'm also a grave of dead feelings

One moment, I'm engulfed in joy
Next a cloud of sorrow embraces me
A boundless fear runs through me
A sense of confidence washes over me

Yet after all this follows
The wash of nothingness, of numbness
Nothing moves for a while
No noise, no movement

Then suddenly, it's chaos.

Unknown Truth

A hesitant feeling follows her
Her confidence ready to shatter
Yet I'm the only one who notices

The fear behind her smiles
The chaos behind her laughs
Emotions twisted and played with

Secrets hidden away
Trust, broken and unknown.
Truth, a sacred, scary truth

Hiding away, running away
I sometimes wonder if
She knows them herself.

Belonging

She runs from place to place
Struggling to find something that fits
She runs and runs and runs
Then suddenly, she stops
Not knowing where to go
Not having anywhere to go
She wants to go back
She cries to go back
Back to where she came from
But that doesn't exist anymore
It's overshadowed by the secrets and lies it stood for
She found everything in this new place
But lost herself
Lost herself too much to find
Now it's all gone.
So, she begs and cries
She begs to go back

A Letter to This World

As the sun drowns past it
A whisp of clouds float over the hilltops.
The whistling of the wind overpowers the birds' melody.
Amidst the city's business, this serenity is all I look for.

Perhaps what I seek lies in the tranquillity of the powerful
    waves
Or rather the peace of the gentle breezes atop
However my answer is long forgotten
As this ethereal scene washes over me.

Online

I fell in love with a photograph
With a voice I'd never heard
With a face I'd never seen
A home I'd never been to.

I fell in love with blue, green words
With pictures spread across my phone,
Notifications covering my lock screen
Audios filling up my storage

I fell in love with bodies I could never hug
With eyes I could never stare into
Smiles I always wanted reciprocate.
Smiles I could never forget.

Shattered Sanity

I feel claustrophobic in your absence
Like this air without you will choke me
The world closes in on me.

The only name that crosses my mind is yours.
My heart chants it over and over
As if that'll bring you back.

I don't care if it drives me insane
I'd do it a 1000 times over
If only it brought you back

The warmth you left in my bed still haunts my dreams.
Your fragrance still lingers in my room
My clothes still have a mark of you in them

It's as if you never left
Yet these empty spaces still daunt me
This grief screams an unheard pain

It begs to tear my limps apart
As though it hasn't already shredded my heart
And shattered my sanity.

Drowning in Love

I always watch her in class.
SEE how her lips curl in a smile
STARS linger around them but
IN her eyes you'll see oceans

YOUR life is nothing compared to the life in her eyes
EYES so full of passion and hope
AND they speak more than she ever does.
SO, I listen more than she ever says

I sink in them,
DROWN deep as I can cause
IN these eyes, I find love and
IT is so strong, it burns me through.

Lies

I love the way you lie
With your lips twisted in a sloppy smile.
Tears held back so easily.

The mockery you put up
As you try to pack up all your feelings
But love, your emotions dangle out of you.

With every smile, I see tears reflected in your eyes
With every tear shed, I hear your mocking laughter
With every lie, your body whispers the truth.

You may fool others with your words
But remember I was the one who taught you these
The bittersweet words you pour out are from the same
script as mine.

A Messed Up World

In this messed up world,
Everyone lives with a sense of melancholia
They like to pretend;
Pretend like the world is in their control

When actually every moment, they're falling apart
Their lives are collapsing and shattering
Breaking them into fragments and pieces,
As they drown in their own mistakes.

Walking around like corpses
They put up a smile
And there it is–yet another act
Just another game in this escape room

The Last Day

Your embrace burns me
Because I know it won't last
Your scarred hands seek out to me
And in an instant, my mind collapses.
A deathly fear runs through my veins
These bloodied hands may not be with me tomorrow.

The clicking of your worn-out sneakers
Runs through my mind every night
I fear this day will be the last I hear them
Your senseless jokes ring in my ears every time I pray
Because really, I reckon today's the last day.
Every day, I fear this day will stand as the last.

Stories of Love

I'd write a million poems for you
If it meant I could keep you alive in these pages
I could immortalise your spirit.
This ink would be heavy with the love you carried.
The words you drew on the walls of my heart will flow
through these pages.

Writing

When I was rather young, I had learnt to
Lock up feelings and fiddle with emotions
So, my teacher had looked over
And said, 'write.'

Write about waves hitting shores or
About the echoes of the mountains.
Write about people you love or
About broken people you couldn't love.

And so I did.
I was a naïve girl
She used to tell me and I would listen.
But writing? I had no one to listen to.

So I wrote and wrote
Until pages were filled and my emotions drained
And before I knew it
I fell in love with writing.

With characters I made up,
Characters that were a part of me.
A world that didn't seem so broken,
A world I could write my way.

Box of Memories

A stained sweatshirt torn at the cuffs
Along with dirty, washed-up boots and old shoes
Jeans with pockets full of gum and change
My costume that still reeks of chlorine

The books with long forgotten bookmarks in them.
Paired with the newspaper wrapped notebooks
And sticky notes with poems sprawled across them
The polaroids and money hidden between my maths
    textbook

The journals gifted on my birthdays
And the broken click pens that wrote in them
That pocket knife & lighter I hid from myself
And the music player that got me through everything.

All of it packed up in a box
And thats about all my story is.

The Storm Inside Me

Your words clashed into my mind
Causing a storm to brew inside me
I hid it all with a smile, and you accepted it
Not doubting it for a second

You kept coming closer and closer
Getting more comfortable with every word
While I was dying inside
Wanting to distance myself and run away

I closed my eyes and the storm begged to be free
I resisted the overwhelming urge to let my tears flow
My mind needed to breathe, but I couldn't let it
Not now at least.

And you never realized it
I hid it and you let it stay hidden
Pretending nothing was wrong
Pretending you weren't wrong.

Romeo, Rose and Juliet

Then Romeo came along
Everything seemed perfect; until it wasn't.
We fought over the silliest things.
'I'm sorry, Juliet, but this won't work out.'

Finally, Rose came along
Nothing seemed perfect, but it was beautiful.
We fought, too, but together; For our rights.
'Will you marry me, Juliet?'

Swearing to never date a boy, I met a girl.
It wasn't like we didn't love each other
We loved each other to death, Forever.
But for Rose and I, forever wasn't even half the time we
    wanted together.

A Messy Blur

I drowned with the screams of everyone around me. I don't wanna be there. Take me out. Take me away. I don't want to stay here. Look at me! Look at what you've done and look at all your mistakes, but most importantly look at my mistakes. Yell at me for them. Praise someone else for the same. Just stop, you're scaring me. My hands are working too fast and my thoughts are even faster. I can't keep going. Stop me. But don't come any further. Breathe, they say. I can't, I can't breathe, I can't let go, I can't stop. Please don't touch me, but don't forget me either. Talk to me, but not too much or else I'll tell you everything. Love me, but don't leave me. Don't leave me like they did. If you do, don't come back. Don't come back and please me and leave me again. I'm tired of everything, I'm tired of myself. Past me was easier. She let people do whatever they wanted, but she didn't care this much. Tell me don't care about it, and I won't. Just tell me once. And once more after that. I'll listen. I can't breathe. Please listen to me. I want to talk to someone. I can't do this. This world is haunting me, telling me to quit. Should I?

First Time

Your words bounced off me.
For the first time, I didn't need you,
Need you to make me happy
Need you to complete me.

I didn't look for parts of you in every person I met.
For the first time, I didn't want you,
Want you to validate me
Want you to make my decisions.

For the first time, our eyes didn't meet
My hands didn't itch to lock yours
My mind didn't beg to let go
And my heart didn't ache

For the first time
It wasn't a lie when I said,
'I am over you,'
'I don't care anymore.'

For the last time, I made the mistake of ever loving you.

Nights

A dying fire,
The last autumn leaf on the trees,
It was a fun night;
But nights end and the sun rises again.

Pieces of broken glass,
A storm brewing nearby
Why is that the night
That lasted?

Tears in those brown eyes
But a smile on his face
Which one do I believe?
The night light glowered over them both.

The oak tree that gave her that scar
Did it really though?
She hides it from the world, from herself.
What really went down that night?

The moon was hidden beneath the clouds
The howling wind singing a soft melody
As the birds sang along
That night, what a beautiful thing it was.

Runaway

Oh, to run away and never return
In the coldness of the grass
And the blankets of mountains and the land.

The low laying wind beneath my feet
And the ever so fascinating sky above me
The fresh breeze that blows around me

The tempting scent of the strawberry trees
And the burned wood,
Along with the call of the ocean waves

Oh, how could I ever turn down,
Something so tempting, something so mesmerising?
But alas, it's all just a dream.

You Could See it All

I wonder what my parents would find
If they had a key to my mind.

Grades, Scores, Marks?
Doubts, denials, self-hate?
Endless days I cried.
All the times I tried.

The fake worlds I've created in my mind
Would you like them?
The imaginary scenarios I stress myself through.
You would see it all.

You would see me sitting in the dark,
Yelling internally,
You would know my smiles are fake,
You would see them too.

You could walk around this mess
Carefully glancing at the things I kept to myself,
Things I was scared to say out loud
Things I would never let you see.

You could see it all.

Moved On

I don't think about you
I don't miss you
I don't care about you
You aren't mine anymore

You live your life
And I live mine
I won't try to be a part of yours
I won't make you a part of mine either

Let's be honest, you weren't the one
Love isn't real and neither is hope
Let's be honest,
I was always a good liar

The Cold (Haiku)

Darkness and despair
Shadows of my dreaded past
Won't leave me free

It calls me out and
A dull feeling passes me
It's that time again

A bleak breeze blows by
The moon hides behind the clouds
It's the call for cold

Dare I say, the cold
Will leave you shivering
Begging for some warmth

The time demeans me
The distance dawns on me
It defeats me too.

Messed Up

I can't explain it
So just watch me and understand.
Say you'll understand but don't.

How do I trust you?
How do I know you care?
Why don't you just tell me?

Lies, jealousy, fake-ness,
Isn't that our relationship?
Don't tell me it's not, because you'll be lying again

I'm messed up
You messed me up, so why not join me?
Be messed up with me.

How can I be sane
When you don't even wanna be friends?
When you found someone else?

The Blame Game

From Barbies to Kardashians,
I lost myself.
The world told me to be perfect,
I listened.

After millions of diets, routines, and exercises
When nothing worked I destroyed myself
I told myself it was for the better
That the world would like me better

I blamed my weight for everything
I blamed my weight for myself
Then I blamed myself for my weight
Together, my heart and my mind played the blame game.

She

Do you like her?
Does she make you smile?
Do you love her laugh?
Her eyes, her jokes, her pickup lines?

Does she stare at you every day?
Does she cry about you every night
Fantasize about you? Dream about you?
Cause I do

Yeah, I do and you never noticed,
You never cared.
You come in like a storm and leave like one
You make me ~~smile~~ cry

Hiraeth

Deep ethereal eyes accompanied by golden brown locks
A smile that glows and brightens the entire class
With a voice that calms and soothes us all
To go with it, a heart that could win anyone

With magic in her soul and sweetness in her voice,
She walks away enchanting everyone around
Her classes will be paradise indeed
Hours go by, and yet they are never enough

From talking about her in the dorm
Smiling over how grateful we are
To whining about her not giving us notes
Her name never goes unspoken

How could it not?
She is after all who we all wished we were
Who we hoped the teachers are;
Someone no one else could ever be.

There's something about her,
Something that makes her so mesmerizing,
For I will never know
How anyone could be so perfect.

Daydreams

Word after word, smile after smile,
They grew more beautiful and deeper

They became my epitome of perfection,
My definition of beauty.

Lost in love, in daydreams,
They became the only clear thought I had.

He

'It doesn't matter anymore'
But the unspoken words
Followed by the secret lingering glances
Say a different story.

The way he says your name
The way you still call him 'yours'
The way both of you think of each other
When 'your song' plays, even now

When everyone's lost in their realities,
The thought pops up–
A wonder of what if,
Of luck, of fate, of hope.

Broken

I look around and all I see is
Everyone drenched in chaos and darkness.
So broken, so tired,
Smiles wiped out of them all

Midst the silence, a storm arose
Fascinated and confused, we followed
It was the only thing we knew; we had
The only guide we ever understood

It all ends where it began,
'I was too broken to be your friend,'
'I was too broken to survive without any,'
In the end, the storm brew over us all

Perfection

With magic in her smile,
Oceans in her eyes
Heaven in a voice and
Divinity in her laugh
She defies my logic
Of perfect not existing;
That in itself is perfection

The World Outside

Blood dripping down from my knuckles
My shirt is covered with tears,
Trying to mask all of my fears.

Unable to bear the present,
Unable to accept the past.
Every second, I hope this breath will be my last.

Scared of the future, mistaken about the present.
The world seems like a foreign land,
Can't I just wait in my little tent?

Blinded by the beliefs of others,
Knowledge passed down by my ancestors,
I sometimes worry if they were wrong

'What if's,' and 'I shouldn't have done that,' defines my
    life
How should I live it, teach me, please?
For I don't know if I'm doing it right.

The slow marching of time leading us to death,
Is it really that slow
Or do we just not care?

Gender, race, colour, caste, shape, and size.
How long are we going to let it define us?
Were we meant to be defined by it?

How long until we break out
And create our own world?
For I don't know if we can survive in yours.

Grades, scores, marks, tests.
Are they really that important?
Teach me something I need because the world outside
    isn't going to ask me my exam results.

Colours

Colours are fascinating
They have a way of describing us

Blue;
Blue is where I belong.
It's where I find peace
Blue is a bittersweet aloofness
It's also what feel most.

Grey;
Grey is how the world is painted the most
Literally, it's the monotonous shades of the city.
Going deeper, it's people.
Grey is the lives they lived.

Red;
I tend to stay away from its fire.
It terrifies me.
Red is hot, contagious
It lives amidst conflicts and quarrels

Yellow
Yellow is rare, an almost negligible shade
It glows in their eyes and reflects in their smiles
Yellow burns with passion and hope
It is kind & forgiving & naïve.

Thank You

Oh, how much it pains me
That I'll never be able to tell you
I'll never be able to thank you,
You saved me

You helped me smile
Made me feel wanted
You appreciated me, loved me
Protected me from this world

You made the scars disappear.

Words and Names Break Me

Incomplete, not enough
Something's always missing
Never as good as the others

Un-included, left out
Use me, replace me, get over me
It's all the same, isn't it?

I want to be free from this constant chaos
I'm suffocated, I'm trapped
I'm trying to be someone else

Someone who is way prettier, way smarter
Way better than me
That's who I'm trying to be

Don't give me solutions to what I'm 1 insecure about,
Give me solutions to my insecurities.
Trust me when I say it's exhausting, it's stressful, it's
    painful

These words haunt me every day
And every night, every sleepless night
Every painful, lonely night.

Sometimes I wonder if they were right
If they understood who I was
Even before I did.

It's Your Game

I don't know what you're waiting for
Your eyes, your smile, your jokes
They all say the same thing.
We all see the way you smile.

The game is yours
All you gotta do is play.
I already lost;
But I know you won't.

I Told the Moon About You

As I lay awake at night, fantasizing about you,
I wished I could tell everyone about you
But I couldn't
So, I told the moon about you.

I told the stars to look over you
I told them all about you
Your sweetness, your sourness
Your ever so free spirit that attracted everyone.

I told them about your personality
I told them about your soul
About your spirit and your aura
I told them all about you

Fascinated, they asked me more
So I told them how you loved me
And let me love you
How you protected me and let me do the same.

The rain too was mesmerised by you
And so were the waves that hit the shore shortly after,
So I told them all about you,
They too fell for you

"Don't let her go," they would tell me
"Never." I would smile,
Thinking about how anyone could ever let you go.
It's you, it always will be.

Not All Men but All Women

I bet you don't carry pepper spray around
I bet you don't carry your keys in between your knuckles.

You haven't memorized all the 'dangerous' areas.
You don't know what time you shouldn't be outside

I bet you don't take various self-defence classes
I bet you don't come back home as soon as the sun goes
    down to keep yourself safe.

You don't have various objects to keep your drink from
    being spiked.
They haven't taught you what to do if someone is trying
    to kidnap you.

I bet you don't have to say that you are dating someone to
    avoid girls.
I bet you aren't scared to leave your house alone.

You don't pull your clothes down every time a woman is
    near
Your clothes don't define your worth.

I bet no one's ever told you to be careful of every damn
    girl.
I bet no one's ever told you, 'girls will be girls,' blaming the
    sexism on you.

Silence is the Loudest Sound

As the light on my phone started getting dimmer
And the bags underneath my eyes got darker
I realized I wasn't as fine as I thought I was.

If I could tell you, I would
But I cant
And it breaks my heart to keep silent.

I'm sorry for all that I've become
Sorry for all that I didn't.
I know how much you wanted them

Happier

They looked happier, their smile brighter
It killed me, even though it shouldn't have
Cause I knew I could never make them smile like that
That I would never be the one.

Your Sight

My scars burn at your sight
My mind forgets to function
Shivers run down my spine
Memories crash into my heart
While your face burns in them.

It's as though I'm frozen, stuck with thoughts
Fragments of our lives together
Stitch themselves in a painful thread
That begins to unwind itself
As I lose myself in your thoughts.

To Be Loved

You know I've always wondered what it would be like
To be loved like poets loved their people
To have songs written in my glory.
To live like Ophelia did,
Or perhaps Juliet or Rose,
To be contained so lovingly in polaroids kept secretly

I've always wondered if you think of me
Whenever you pick up Yeats' books.
Or when you hear cheesy love songs on radios
When you see unrealistic romcom couples
Or when you lay awake at daybreak,
I know I always do.

Selfish

You're selfish, you know
To leave before I could.

You're selfish that you let me fall
Knowing that I'd never be able to get back up
You're selfish for picking me up
Just for me to fall even harder

You're selfish that you never let anyone but yourself
See this beauty that burns within you.

You're selfish, you're greedy, you're an asshole
But you know, even I'm not convinced by these words.
Cause really, they're just excuses for me to be selfish
And have you all for myself

A Spring Without You

This spring without you isn't of despair
It's of so much nostalgia, it's almost tough to bear.
My heart remains heavy with memories we made and
My mind rings with all the promises we laid.

The empty chairs in the room daunt me
Yet this hollowness will cease to haunt me.
Cause this spring without you is one of love,
A love always with us, no matter how many places we
    move.

I write this, without you by my side
With immense joy but also the sorrow that I fail to hide
But I'd write a million poems more
If all these memories I could store.

Of Chaos and of Love

You're an outburst of hatred, of coldness
Of everything we've learnt not to be.
You're the missing pieces of a puzzle
I lost long back in a box under some books.

You're an arrow shot right at my moral compass
Deflecting it and almost breaking it.
You're everything my friends warned me against
Everything I stand against

Yet you're everything I want.
You're goddamn wild storm
You aren't like those dream boys in books,
You're neither funny nor warm.

You're a messed up wreck
A control freak with a dark humour
A chaotic mind with a sadist heart.
You're the epitome of an obnoxious, ornery person.

But damn, do you feel right?
You mess with my mind
But hey, atleast that way,
You're always on my mind.

It's an interesting thing honestly;
To be loved and hated by the same person.
Cause you're a damn mess
But so am I.

We Cry on the Same Floor

It's not like I don't understand
I understand you're going through pain.
I understand that nothing feels right.

I understand, I really do
But I too, feel stuck in this overwhelming world.
I too, spend hours wailing my eyes out

Sitting against the bathroom wall
You & I have cried on the same floor
We suffer together

It's not our generation gap
Or even our sorrow that divides us
It's merely a wall between our rooms.

Yet this distance seems too far
And every conversation it grows
But if we hate it so much, why do we let it grow?

We miss the same people.
We suffer together
Then why do we make each other suffer?

Cause, in the end,
We both take turns in crying
On the same bathroom floor.

Author Bio

Born and brought up in the town of Darjeeling, Tanishi Agarwal is a young writer studying in the south of the country. She started writing poems and stories two years ago, when she was 13. Through poetry, she desires to bring life to her thoughts, emotions, and ideas. In this narrative anthology, Tanishi expressed her thoughts and feelings about the experiences she has had and the problems she has faced. A year back, this was what she needed, and if someone else feels the same way, she hopes this reaches them.